If I could work instead of play,
I'd get up early every day.

I'd drive a bus and
shout, "Fares, please!"

For Xan and Alice
T.B.

For Alex and Rosie
C.W.

Fun-to-Read Picture Books have been
grouped into three approximate readability
levels by Bernice and Cliff Moon. Yellow
books are suitable for beginners; red books
for readers acquiring first fluency; blue
books for more advanced readers.

This book has been assessed as Stage 6
according to *Individualised Reading*, by
Bernice and Cliff Moon, published by
The Centre for the Teaching of Reading,
University of Reading
School of Education.

First published 1987 by
Walker Books Ltd
184-192 Drummond Street
London NW1 3HP

First printed 1987
Printed and bound by
L.E.G.O., Vicenza, Italy

British Library Cataloguing in Publication Data
Blacker, Terence
If I could work – (Fun-to-read picture books)
I. Title II. Winn, Chris III. Series
823'.914[J] PZ7

ISBN 0-7445-0551-8

IF I COULD
WORK

Written by
Terence Blacker
Illustrated by
Chris Winn

WALKER BOOKS
LONDON

I'd rescue cats
from the tops of trees.

I'd be an inventor and
make lots of toys,

I'd play the guitar and make too much noise.

I'd be the world's
favourite TV star,

I'd be a doctor and
make children say, "Aaaah."

I'd open a shop
with sweets on the shelf,
When no one was looking
I'd eat them myself.

I'd smile at people
as they drove past,

I'd stop them if
they went too fast.

I'd be an incredibly silly clown,
I'd make people laugh
when my trousers fell down.

I'd be the first child
to go to the moon,
I'd tell my parents
I'd be back soon.

And I'd fly back home
at the end of the day,

I'd really much rather work than play.